**Meditating
for
Success**

Meditating for Success

Paul Meier, M.D.

BAKER BOOK HOUSE
Grand Rapids, Michigan 49506

Copyright 1985 by
Baker Book House Company

ISBN: 0-8010-6207-1

Third printing, July 1989

Printed in the United States of America

Unless indicated otherwise, Scripture
quotations are from the King James Version.
Other translations cited are from the
New American Standard Bible (NASB)
copyrighted by the Lockman Foundation,
1960, 1962, 1963, 1968, 1971, 1972, 1973, 1975, 1977,
and from The New International
Version (NIV), © 1978 by New York
International Bible Society.

We wish to thank Jane Mack for her careful work in editing this book.

Contents

Meditating for Success   11

Case Study
    Seminarians and "Renewing Your Mind"   19

Case Study
    A Troubled Christian Finds Help   29

God's Perspective on Good Mental Health   41

Some Recent Research on Meditation   47

A Suggested Method for Scripture Meditation   57

Meditate on the Lord

Do you not know? Have you not heard?

The Lord is the everlasting God the creator of the ends of the earth.

He will not grow tired or weary,

and his understanding no one can fathom.

He gives strength to the weary

and increases the power of the weak.

*Even youths grow tired and weary,
    and young men stumble and fall;
but those who hope in the Lord will
    renew their strength.*

*They will soar on wings like eagles;
they will run and not grow weary,
they will walk and not be faint.*

Isaiah 40:28-31, NIV

Meditating for Success

To prepare myself for a role in society as a Christian psychiatrist, I undertook college studies, a M.S. Degree in Human Physiology, a M.D. from medical school, psychiatric residency training in two different programs, and theological coursework from two evangelical seminaries. During those busy years of preparation, I was equipped with many techniques and "short-cuts" for bringing human beings relief from their own anxieties, depression, phobias, fears, insecurities, and other kinds of emotional and/or physical pain. Among the many tools I learned to use, by far the most valuable one for attaining spiritual well-being is Scripture meditation.

Since man is a holistic being, his spiritual, psychological and physical faculties are complexly intertwined. Every aspect of man's nature affects him as a whole

Meditating for Success

being. Daily meditation on the principles of life passed on from man's loving Creator is more important for his holistic health than food or sex or any other factor.

One primary reason why Scripture meditation is so vital for holistic health is this: God's thought patterns and values are in sharp contrast to mankind's. Man is a totally depraved being, possessing selfish and ultimately self-destructive thought patterns and behavior. Show me a natural man, untaught in God's principles, and I'll show you a man who suffers from emotional pain. I'll show you a man who experiences the guilt and discomfort of a God-vacuum. I'll show you a man who is unconsciously fighting and struggling for a sense of significance and who is using worldly ways (e.g., sexual fantasy, materialism, power struggles, prestige, etc.) in a vain attempt to attain significance, all

Meditating for Success

of which ultimately fail. The ways of the world may bring temporary relief, like Bandaids on open flesh wounds, but not ultimate relief from man's inner awareness of his insignificance apart from God.

The billionaire, John D. Rockefeller, was once asked by a reporter how much money it would take to make him happy. John D. scratched his chin and thought for a moment, then replied with sincerity, "Just a little bit more!" When the search for relief results in an appetite for sexual affairs, power, money, or prestige, the hunger is never satisfied. There is constantly the desire to have "just a little bit more." Sadly, even that "little bit more" satisfies man only a short time. The gnawing desire for identity, self-worth, and significance soon returns with ever greater intensity.

Man's ultimate sense of holistic well-being can come *only* from a personal rela-

Meditating for Success

tionship with God through Jesus Christ. But man needs more than salvation for joy and peace in his daily existence. Many of my anxious, depressed, and even suicidal patients are born-again believers who have not yet been taught how to appropriate personally God's thought patterns and behavioral principles outlined in the Bible. Rather, they have been misinformed, and misguided by parents, peers, and frequently even by their churches. They have learned to think negative, self-critical, other-critical, destructive thoughts. They have become accustomed to behavior patterns that ultimately result in increased guilt, insecurity, and feelings of insignificance.

Give me, O Lord,

a steadfast heart
  which no unworthy thought can
    drag downward;

an unconquered heart
  which no tribulation can wear out;

an upright heart
  which no unworthy purpose may
    tempt aside.

Bestow on me also, O Lord God,

understanding to know thee,

diligence to seek thee,

wisdom to find thee, and

a faithfulness that may finally
  embrace thee.

Thomas A'Kempis 1379-1471

Case Study
Seminarians and "Renewing Your Mind"

A few years ago I conducted an extensive research study on seminary students from a midwestern seminary. The research included psychological testing (using the Minnesota Multiphasic Personality Inventory, or MMPI), and an extensive Spiritual Life Questionnaire. The completed psychological test results were divided into three groups:

Group A: Those with exceptionally excellent mental health and maturity.

Group B: Those with apparently normal mental health and maturity.

Group C: Those who were still struggling with statistically significant psychological conflicts and emotional pain.

I then ran statistical analyses comparing their mental health/maturity factor with each factor on their Spiritual Life Questionnaire.

As the results were coming in, I was initially surprised and disappointed. Those seminary students who had been Christians for many years were only slightly healthier and happier than those who had accepted Christ in the past one or two years. The difference was not even statistically significant.

However, my disappointment turned to joy. I learned one of the most valuable lessons of my life when I found the factor that made the difference. That factor was Scripture meditation. Students who had practiced almost daily Scripture meditation for *three years or longer* came out, statistically, significantly healthier and happier than students who did not meditate on Scripture daily. They also came out, statistically, significantly healthier and

Case Study: Seminarians and "Renewing Your Mind"

---

happier than students who had meditated on Scripture daily for *less than three years*. The significance level on the various psychological scales varied from the 0.05 level (meaning only one chance in twenty that it was a coincidence) to the 0.001 level (meaning only one chance in a thousand that it was a coincidence).

The valuable lessons I learned from this research could best be summarized as follows:

1 ❈ Even though trusting Christ is all that is needed to obtain eternal life, experiencing the abundant life Christ promised (John 10:10) and experiencing the fruit of the Spirit (love, joy, peace, patience, kindness, goodness, faithfulness, gentleness and self-control) rather than bitterness, depression and anxiety depends on a renewing of one's mind.

Meditating for Success

2 Renewing of the mind can come from various sources, such as confrontations about personal blind-spots from loving friends, therapy with a Christian professional counselor, convictions from the Holy Spirit, encounters with Scriptural principles in sermons or seminars, and daily meditation on Scripture.

3 Renewing of the mind is a *continual process, progressive sanctification,* requiring *continual* (preferably daily) input from God's Word.

4 Daily meditation on Scripture (with personal application) is the most effective means of obtaining personal joy, peace, and emotional maturity.

**Case Study:
Seminarians
and
"Renewing Your Mind"**

---

5 It takes, on the average, about three years of daily Scripture meditation to bring about enough change in a person's thought patterns and behavior to produce statistically superior mental health and happiness.

6 *None* of the students in Group C (those with statistically significant psychological conflicts) were presently meditating on Scripture daily, although some were *reading* their Bibles regularly as a textbook for their classes.

7 *All* of the students who had meditated on Scripture daily (or almost daily) for three years or longer were in Group A or Group B with most being in Group A (superior in mental health, happiness, and maturity).

I rejoice in following your statutes
  as one rejoices in great riches.
I meditate on your precepts
  and consider your ways.
I delight in your decrees;
  I will not neglect your word.
The law from your mouth is more
    precious to me
  than thousands of pieces of silver
    and gold.
How sweet are your promises to my
    taste,
  sweeter than honey to my mouth!
Because I love your commands more
    than gold,
more than pure gold, and because I
    consider

*all your precepts right,
   I hate every wrong path.
Your statutes are wonderful;
   therefore I obey them.
The entrance of your words gives
      light;
   it gives understanding to the simple.
Trouble and distress have come upon
      me,
   but your commands are my delight.
Your statutes are forever right;
   give me understanding that I may
      live.*

*Selections from
Psalm 119, NIV*

Case Study
A Troubled Christian Finds Help

Mary D. was treated by my partners and me in a psychiatry unit of a general hospital. She admitted herself to our unit because of suicidal depression. She was thirty years old, was married to a loving Christian husband, had two healthy children, and was financially secure but not wealthy. She attended a very good local church, where her husband was a church officer. There were no current external circumstances that would appear to make Mary suicidally depressed. <u>Her conflicts, like those of most humans, were within herself and stemmed from early childhood thought and behavior patterns.</u>

Mary had suffered from bouts of depression most of her life. For several months prior to her hospitalization, Mary experienced increasing anxiety, depression, insomnia, loss of appetite, weight loss, loss of sexual drive, loss of energy, early morning

Meditating for Success

headaches, stomachaches, crying spells, feelings of hopelessness, infections, and a fear of losing her mind. She had absolutely no insight into what might be causing her psychological and physical symptoms. She was hoping to find out that it was hypoglycemia or some hormonal deficiency, since this would be less embarrassing than to have to admit to her friends that she was having psychological conflicts. However, thorough medical evaluation by her family physician revealed no physical abnormalities that would cause such symptoms. Her family physician recommended psychiatric consultation, which Mary took as an insult. Unwilling to search within herself, Mary grew progressively worse. One evening she suddenly lost touch with reality, thought her husband was plotting to kill her, and left her bed to get a knife to kill her husband in

**Case Study:
A Troubled
Christian
Finds Help**

"self-defense." Fortunately, he woke up and prevented her from killing him. He was shocked to find out that she now believed she was God, and that he was the devil. She "heard" both God and demons speaking to her in audible voices (auditory hallucinations). Her husband called their pastor, an experienced counselor. The pastor and his wife immediately came to Mary's house. Together, the three of them (husband, pastor and pastor's wife) persuaded Mary to meet me at the hospital. After committing herself to the hospital, Mary again became violent, condemning the nursing staff to hell, and had to be physically restrained by six nurses and aides.

I gave Mary moderate doses of a major antipsychotic medication. Within thirty-six hours Mary was over her psychosis and had no more delusions or hallucinations (voices), but was very depressed and extremely frightened by the fact that she had almost killed her loving husband while in her psychotic state.

After regaining her sanity through the help of medication, Mary willingly began daily psychotherapy. It soon became obvious that Mary's problems stemmed from early childhood. She was the only daughter of a controlling, critical, insecure mother and a passive father. She had two younger brothers who seemed to have adjusted reasonably well. (Note: Insecure mothers nearly always are most critical of the oldest daughter, and insecure fathers of the oldest son, because of a mechanism known as projection, which is described in Matthew 7:1-5.)

Mary's mother was overly critical of Mary growing up, so Mary was filled with constant self-critical messages as an adult. Mary's mother was legalistic and rigid: so

**Case Study:
A Troubled
Christian
Finds Help**

Mary, as an adult, was filled with continual false guilt over minor things that most people would ignore. Mary's mother did not tolerate little Mary sharing her anger or other feelings; so Mary, as an adult, continually repressed her emotions, denied her anger, and even felt guilty for having these normal emotions. Mary's mother overly controlled young Mary; so Mary, as an adult, was afraid to make independent decisions or to be assertive.

At the same time, however, Mary was in many ways a wonderful person who was very kind and thoughtful to her husband, children, and friends. And yet Mary had significant emotional pain and feelings of insignificance because of her negative thought patterns, legalistic false-guilt, over-dependence on others to make her decisions, and fear of becoming aware of her repressed hostility toward her mother, who she consciously loved dearly. The truth was carefully, step-by-step, revealed to Mary in the hospital. Showing her too much truth too quickly would have tipped her back into hearing "voices" and having paranoid delusions. Antipsychotic medications were continued to keep her brain's dopamine levels balanced to help prevent another psychosis. Mary's internal conflicts (spiritual and psychological) had also resulted in all of the physiological accompaniments of depression (fatigue, insomnia, loss of appetite, loss of sex drive, etc.). These symptoms come only when the conflicts are severe enough to cause depletion of serotonin and norepinephrine, two essential brain amines. Therefore, antidepressant medications were also given to speed up her physiological recovery.

The primary daily homework Mary was given was meditating on Scriptures re-

Case Study: A Troubled Christian Finds Help

lated to her problems, such as self-worth (Psalm 139), legalism (Ephesians 4:26 and Galatians) and unconscious vengeful attitudes (Romans 12). Through meditation on Scripture and daily therapeutic confrontation with the truth about her resentment toward her mother, Mary was able to become aware of her intense but hidden bitterness toward her mother. She was then able for the first time in her life to forgive her mother. She learned that her buried emotions and conflicts had resulted in biochemical changes in her brain, resulting in depression and even psychosis. She learned that even though modern medicines could restore these chemicals to normal quite rapidly, it would take right thinking, right attitudes, and right behavior to keep these brain amines normal in the future, so she would not need any medicines six months down the road.

Meditating for Success

She was encouraged to meditate on Scripture daily to facilitate the renewing process. She was also encouraged to continue outpatient therapy for a year or so to be sure she was not misinterpreting Scripture negatively and to receive continuing encouragement and support in her new ways of thinking. Within several weeks of hospitalization, Mary was over her psychosis and her depression. She continued to progress in outpatient therapy and is now living a very happy, abundant Christian life and enjoying the fruit of the Spirit.

From this true example, you can see that the spiritual, emotional, and physiological aspects of a person are complexly interwoven. Even Mary's infections were the result of decreased antibodies because of lymphocytes that were suppressed by her own stress hormones.

Some well-intentioned but uninformed

**Case Study:
A Troubled
Christian
Finds Help**

pastors might have tried exorcism of Mary's "demons" and blamed her life-long insanity (which she would have suffered without prompt treatment) on her lack of faith.* Some paramedical quacks would try to convince her she had hypoglycemia or some nutritional disorder and persuaded her to spend hundreds of wasted dollars on megavitamins, natural foods, etc. Other well-intentioned but naive friends might have convinced her she had cancer and sent her for laetrile treatment in Mexico. Others might refer Mary to an astrologist for help. We are living in a hysterical society today that is almost as embedded in native myths as were people who lived during the Dark Ages. Only Mary's growing insight concerning her re-

---

*Demons do exist, since the Bible says they do, but I believe demons are working in more subtle ways today.

pressed feelings coupled with her meditation on God's inerrant Word will produce life-long joy, peace, and a sense of significance for this troubled Christian.

God's Perspective on Good Mental Health

When I was ten years old, my mother helped me to memorize Psalm 1. Psalm 1 teaches us much about renewing our minds. Every Christian who is interested in good mental health as God perceives it should carefully reflect on what each line of this psalm means for him or her in daily living:

> *How blessed is the man who does not*
> *   walk in the counsel of the wicked,*
> *Nor stand in the path of sinners,*
> *Nor sit in the seat of scoffers!*
> *But his delight is in the law of the Lord,*
> *And in His law he meditates day and*
> *   night.*
> *And he will be like a tree firmly*
> *   planted by streams of water,*
> *Which yields its fruit in its season,*
> *And its leaf does not wither;*
> *And in whatever he does, he prospers.*

Meditating for Success

> *The wicked are not so,*
> *But they are like chaff which the wind drives away.*
> *Therefore the wicked will not stand in the judgment,*
> *Nor sinners in the assembly of the righteous.*
> *For the Lord knows the way of the righteous*
> *But the way of the wicked will perish.*
> *(NASB)*

This psalm clearly teaches a direct relationship between Scripture meditation and the person who enjoys God-given happiness.

*When in the night I meditate
 On mercies multiplied,
My grateful heart inspires my tongue
 To bless the Lord, my Guide.*

*Forever in my thought the Lord
 Before my face shall stand;
Secure, unmoved, I shall remain,
 With him at my right hand.*

*My inmost being thrills with joy
 And gladness fills my breast;
Because on him my trust is stayed,
 My flesh in hope shall rest.*

*Metrical version of
Psalm 16*

Some Recent Research on Meditation

Literally hundreds of research articles, especially in the past twenty years, have proven a very close correlation between psychological stress and physical illnesses of nearly every kind. It is not my purpose here to give a lengthy summary of those findings. Rather, I hope to encourage the reader to improve his or her own existence and growth toward Christ-like maturity by learning more about meditation.

One of the most interesting secular studies on the value of "meditation" *per se* was conducted in 1974 by Herbert Benson, M.D., a professor at Harvard Medical School. Dr. Benson wrote an article in the *Harvard Business Review*, July-August, 1974 (pp. 40-60), titled "Your innate asset for combating stress." He chose that journal (rather than a medical journal) so that he could help overworked businessmen and women reduce their stress levels and

Meditating for Success

thereby prolong and enjoy life. In his article, Dr. Benson, a cardiologist, describes some of the physiologic changes that take place during stress, including elevated blood pressure.

In our everyday lives, whenever we experience a stress that requires behavioral adjustment our body physiology responds with what Dr. Walter B. Cannon labeled the "fight-or-flight" response. Dr. Benson notes that "this response is characterized by coordinated increases in metabolism, oxygen consumption, blood pressure, heart rate, rate of breathing, amount of blood pumped by the heart, and amount of blood pumped to the skeletal muscles" (*Ibid*, p. 50). This response is an integrated physiologic mechanism, mediated by epinephrine and norepinephrine (also called adrenalin and noradrenalin), leading to coordinated activity by the sympathetic

Some Recent Research on Meditation

nervous system. The response helps us to either "fight" or "flee" in situations that we perceive to be potentially dangerous emotionally or physically.

Dr. Benson notes that "although the fight-or-flight response is still a necessary and useful physiologic feature for survival, the stresses of today's society have led to its excessive elicitation." This can lead to chronic high blood pressure, which predisposes man to heart attacks or strokes. These two diseases account for over 50 percent of all deaths each year in the United States. Dr. Benson estimates that from 15 to 33 percent of Americans suffer from varying degrees of high blood pressure, and many of them are business executives.

In his article, Dr. Benson compares the physiological benefits of various types of meditation, including progressive relaxation, autogenic training, Zen, yoga and

Meditating for Success

transcendental meditation. Most of these meditation techniques, judging from his extensive research, proved to be physiologically beneficial and had an opposite effect of the fight-or-flight response on such variables as oxygen consumption, respiratory rate, heart rate, blood pressure, and muscle tension. The meditation techniques also generally tended to increase brain alpha waves on EEG. Dr. Benson proposes his own method of meditation, which he calls the "relaxation response." He states that for any meditation techniques to elicit these beneficial physiological responses, it must have four basic elements:

1 A quiet environment (no noise or music).

**Some Recent
Research
on Meditation**

---

2 A mental device (repeated thought the word on a single topic or word to free oneself from externally-oriented thoughts or worries).

3 A passive attitude (passively disregarding the distracting thoughts that tend to intrude on the mind, but not actively fighting them, since this often tends to make them worse).

4 A comfortable position (to reduce muscular effort to a minimum).

Some years ago I attended *The Midwest Symposium on Meditation-Related Therapies* in St. Louis, Missouri. One of the guest lecturers was Dr. Herbert Benson. In his lecture (presented on October 28, 1977), Dr.

Meditating for Success

Benson revealed that, since his research article on meditating through the relaxation response had appeared (in 1974), Harvard psychiatrists had also found the same physiologically beneficial responses in Christians who pray meditatively or who meditate on single principles or phrases from the Bible.

Medical patients who had various degrees of high blood pressure were taught to meditate twice a day for twenty-five weeks. They experienced an average decrease of blood pressure of 8mmHg systolic pressure and 5mmHg diastolic pressure. The higher the patient's initial blood pressure, the greater the potential drop in blood pressure. These benefits were obtained by using either Benson's method or Christian meditation. In fact, Benson stated that his "religious patients" had the greatest compliance to his relaxation techniques to lower their blood pressure.

Some Recent Research on Meditation

Dr. Benson warned that meditating while lying prone does not work well. Too many people fall asleep. He recommended that aspirants sit up in a comfortable chair. Dr. Benson also noted that the kneeling position works equally well if not better than most other meditative positions. People who kneel find it easier to stay awake.

He pointed out that it is no longer popular in our society to pray and meditate once or twice a day, as it was in past decades. This fact may provide one reason why hardening of the arteries is becoming an increasing problem for Americans at increasingly younger ages.

A Suggested Method for Scripture Meditation

This is a method of Scripture meditation that I recommend for my psychiatric patients as well as use myself:

1. Go to a quiet place. Occasionally vary the pace by going out alone to a lake or stream.

2. Find a comfortable position (but preferably not lying down prone).

3. Relax your whole mind and body, including the various muscle groups.

4. Pray that the Holy Spirit will guide you into applicable truths as you read God's Word.

5. Read consecutively through the Bible, but don't place any legalistic guidelines on yourself (e.g., four chapters a day, etc.)

6. When you come to a verse that jumps out at you, offers you real comfort or otherwise confronts you with a needed behavioral change, **stop and meditate on that verse or even a phrase within the verse for several minutes.**

7. As you meditate on that single principle from Scripture, **think of ways to appropriate personally that principle into your everyday behavior.** Passively resist other unrelated thoughts and worries that intrude on your mind.

A Suggested Method for Scripture Meditation

If Christians would meditate in such a manner for ten to thirty minutes morning and evening, they will probably experience the following successful results:

1. Greater knowledge of Scripture and understanding of who God is.

2. Greater personal application of Scriptural principles.

3. Lower blood pressure and other beneficial, physiologic responses.

4. Longer life of usefulness here on earth for the Lord.

5. Greater ability to passively resist anxieties of the day, even during non-meditative time.

Meditating for Success

6. Greater awareness of unconscious truths about personal blindspots as one becomes less afraid of the truth and one's mind puts up less resistance to the truth.

7. Greater success in family life and business.

These are no small gains. With the power of the Holy Spirit prompting us, we can experience the renewing of our minds on a daily basis. <u>The key is to meditate on God's Word so that we think God's thoughts.</u>

Finally, brethren, whatsoever things are true, whatsoever things are honest, whatsoever things are just, whatsoever things are pure, whatsoever things are lovely, whatsoever things are of good report: if there be any virtue, and if there

A Suggested Method for Scripture Meditation

---

be any praise, think [meditate] on these things.

Those things, which ye have both learned, and received, and heard, and seen in me, do: and the God of peace shall be with you.

The Apostle Paul, A.D. 64
Philippians 4:8-9